Dear Parent:
Your child's love of reading starts here!

Every child learns to read in a different way and at his or her own speed. Some go back and forth between reading levels and read favorite books again and again. Others read through each level in order. You can help your young reader improve and become more confident by encouraging his or her own interests and abilities. From books your child reads with you to the first books he or she reads alone, there are I Can Read Books for every stage of reading:

SHARED READING
Basic language, word repetition, and whimsical illustrations, ideal for sharing with your emergent reader

BEGINNING READING
Short sentences, familiar words, and simple concepts for children eager to read on their own

READING WITH HELP
Engaging stories, longer sentences, and language play for developing readers

READING ALONE
Complex plots, challenging vocabulary, and high-interest topics for the independent reader

I Can Read Books have introduced children to the joy of reading since 1957. Featuring award-winning authors and illustrators and a fabulous cast of beloved characters, I Can Read Books set the standard for beginning readers.

A lifetime of discovery begins with the magical words "I Can Read!"

Visit www.icanread.com for information on enriching your child's reading experience.

Visit www.zonderkidz.com/icanread for more faith-based I Can Read! titles from Zonderkidz.

The LORD gave the fish a command.
And it spit Jonah up onto dry land.
—*Jonah 2:10*

ZONDERKIDZ

The Beginner's Bible Jonah and the Giant Fish
Copyright © 2007 by Zondervan
Illustrations © 2019 by Zondervan

An **I Can Read Book**

Requests for information should be addressed to:

Zonderkidz, 3900 Sparks Drive SE, Grand Rapids, Michigan 49546

Softcover ISBN 978-0-310-76044-3
Hardcover ISBN 978-0-310-74328-6
Ebook ISBN 978-0-310-76038-2

Library of Congress Cataloging-in-Publication Data

Title: Jonah and the giant fish.
Description: Grand Rapids, Michigan : Zonderkidz, 2019. | Series: The
    beginner's Bible | Audience: Ages 0 to 4 | Summary: "A faithful
    retelling of the Old Testament story, Jonah and the Giant Fish features
    vibrant art and will show children that God forgives us like he forgave
    Jonah, and will always love us even when we make poor choices"--
    Provided by publisher.
Identifiers: LCCN 2019002447 | ISBN 9780310760443 (paperback)
Subjects: LCSH: Jonah (Biblical prophet)--Juvenile literature. | Bible
    stories, English--Jonah.
Classification: LCC BS580.J55 J627 2019 | DDC 224/.9209505--dc23
LC record available at https://lccn.loc.gov/2019002447

Illustrator: Denis Alonso

Jonah and the Giant Fish

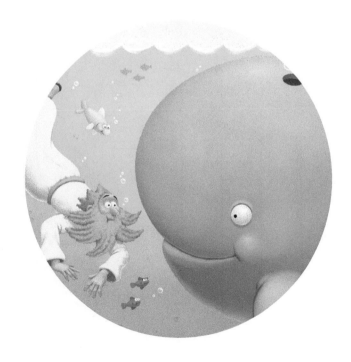

Jonah told people about God.

One day, God told Jonah
to go on a trip.

God said, "People in Nineveh are doing bad things. Please go there and talk to them."

Jonah was not happy.

He did not want to go.

So he ran away!

Jonah talked to some men.
"Please let me sail away
with you."

The boat went out to sea.

It went right into a storm!

The wind blew and blew.

The waves went up and down,
up and down.

The men were scared.

"Where is Jonah?" they called.

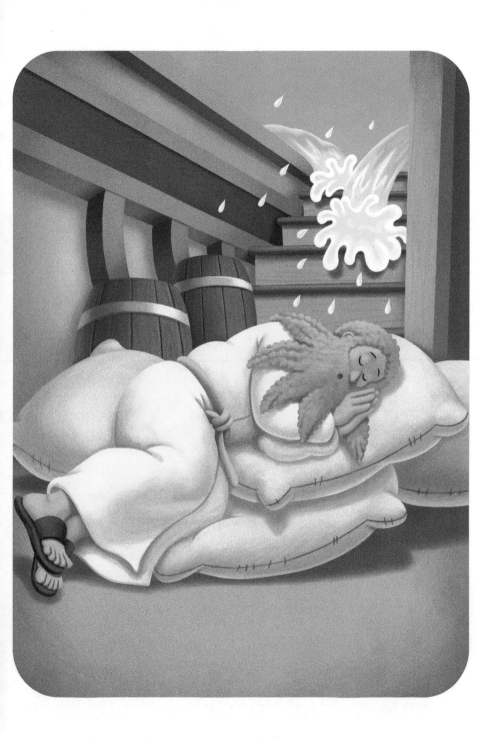

Jonah was taking a nap.

"Get up, Jonah," they said.

"We are in big trouble!

Say a prayer for us!"

"God is upset. I ran away from him!" Jonah said.

"He wants me to go back. He wants me to go to Nineveh."

"How do we stop this storm?"
asked the men.

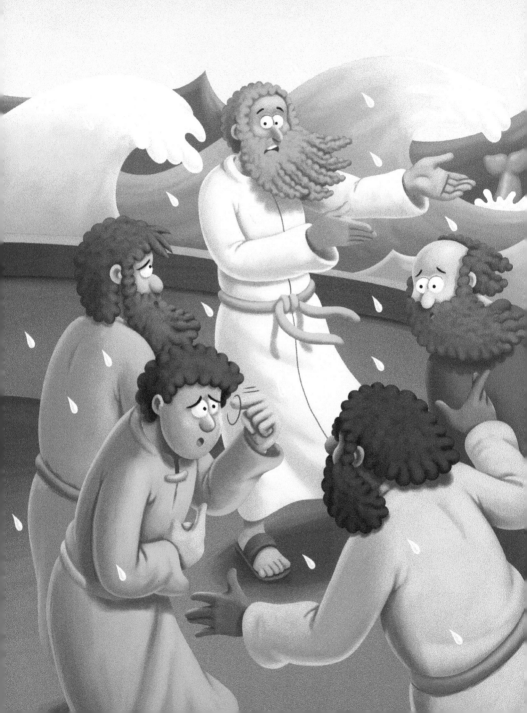

Jonah said,
"You must throw me
into the water."

The men tossed Jonah
into the water.

The storm stopped.

The sea was calm!

But up from the water
swam a big fish.

The fish swallowed Jonah.

Jonah sat in the big fish
for three days
and three nights.

"I am sorry I ran away.
Thank you, God, for saving
me," said Jonah.

Then God said, "Big fish!
Put Jonah back on dry land!"

God said, "Jonah, go to
Nineveh. Tell the people
to stop doing bad things."

This time Jonah was brave.
He knew God was with him.

Jonah went to talk

to the people of Nineveh.

Jonah told the people,
"Stop doing bad things!"

They listened to Jonah.

God forgave Jonah.

God forgave the people.

He loves all his people.